Riley —

Good luck with

I hope this helps.

SHUT UP!

*A Quick & Dirty Guide to Decreasing Teacher Talk
and Increasing Student Talk in the Classroom*

Deb Teitelbaum, PhD, NBCT

CONTENTS

CHAPTER 1

Why Teachers Should Talk Less

Imagine you're a fly on the wall in a Senior Composition class. Today's lesson is how to write effective introductory paragraphs. The teacher is a well-intentioned, energetic young woman who recently attended a workshop at the University of Chicago where she learned a useful formula for writing introductions. She cannot wait to share it with her students. She begins explaining the process:

"How many of you were taught to start your papers with 'an attention getter'"?

A few hands go up. A few heads nod. Mostly the students just sit and stare. Perhaps they are paying attention. Perhaps they are merely giving the appearance of paying attention.

"Well, you *do* want to get your reader's attention. So can I start my paper with, 'BOOBS!!'"?

Several students laugh. A few check in, realize, sadly, that there are no actual boobs, and return to their happy places.

"Unless my paper is about, maybe, a controversial breast cancer treatment, that's not an appropriate beginning. What you want to do is get your readers on your side. You want to make a statement that pretty much everyone can agree with, a statement that gets people nodding the way the women in Oprah Winfrey's audiences do when one of her guests says something profound. You know that slow nod of agreement? That's what you want. This part of the introduction is called 'establishing common ground.' Kyle, write that down."

Kyle reluctantly returns from his mental vacation and seems surprised to find himself holding a pen. He writes in his notebook, "Common ground." He has no idea what this means. The teacher does not realize this, and Kyle does not care.

This process continues for approximately fifteen minutes as she explains the second and third portions of an introduction (destabilizing condition and thesis) and then models writing an introduction using this process.

Finally, it's the students' turn.

"Okay, I want you to try using this formula to write your own introductory paragraph."

Students begin working with varying degrees of enthusiasm and competence.

"Ms. T., can you come over here?" She does. "I don't think I get what you mean by 'common ground.'"

She repeats the explanation she gave several minutes earlier and wonders, uncharitably, "Where the hell have you been for the last 20 minutes?"

"Ms. T., what's a destabilizing condition again?"

"It's a way of suggesting that the common ground might not always be true."

"Okay. Wait! What's common ground again?"

The above scenario is not atypical. Every day across this great land of ours, one can hear hundreds of thousands of teachers asking, "What did I *just* say?!" And in most cases, this question is entirely rhetorical. Our students have no idea what we just said.

Now, we can debate whose fault that is, but that's not a very profitable use of our time. Ultimately, if something is to change in the classroom, we must change first.`

THE CONSEQUENCES OF TOO MUCH TEACHER TALK

When teacher talk dominates the classroom, students' responsibilities are limited to listening and taking notes. Only the most mentally disciplined of students can remain fully engaged with the material under these conditions. A wealth of negative repercussions is associated with excessive teacher talk.

Students Tend to Learn Less. It is the rare teacher who can monopolize classroom discourse without becoming a source of tedium. Bored students become disengaged students. Now, while it is true that a student who is engaged is not necessarily learning anything, it is also true that a student who is disengaged is *definitely* not learning anything.

Ongoing assessment is made more difficult. Presenting large amounts of information via direct instruction limits a teacher's ability to determine whether and how much the students understand. During lectures, even great teachers tend to rely on student self-reports of their understanding, asking, "Got it?" or "Are there any questions before I move on?" Doug Lemov (2010) noted that "often, students don't know they missed something because, well, they missed it" (p. 31). A great deal of what Lemov calls "targeted questioning" must accompany a lecture if the teacher is to accurately assess student understanding.

Critical thinking is diminished. Targeted questioning has its limits. The initiation-response-evaluation model of classroom interaction again limits the student to a fairly passive role. The teacher decides who talks, when and for how long. Students are asked to take no responsibility for their learning or their choices. In a series of briefs, the Partnership for 21st Century

Learning emphasized communication, critical thinking, creativity, and collaboration—their 4 Cs—as "essential to prepare all students for the challenges of work, life, and citizenship . . . as well as ensure ongoing innovation in our economy and the health of our democracy." Far from developing the 4 C's, students subjected to excessive teacher talk become, at best, the 3 P's: passive, patient, and polite.

CLASSROOM DISCOURSE AND THE ACHIEVEMENT/OPPORTUNITY GAP

When students don't use the vocabulary we teach them, they never really take ownership of those words (Fisher, Frey, & Rothenberg, 2008; Weimer, 2012). The need for intentional and explicit language instruction is even greater for students who are new to English or who have grown up in impoverished households.

Hart & Risley (2003) found that, by the time they were three years old, children in welfare homes had heard, on average, 30-40 million fewer words than their higher SES peers. This auditory deficit has a domino effect on literacy. The ability to "sound out" a word depends upon students recognizing a particular combination of letter sounds as a word they have heard previously.

Two equally capable students, one from a language-rich home, another from a home where fewer words are used, will have markedly different achievement in language arts. In many cases, poor and minority students are classified as learning disabled, not because they cannot read but because they have not yet developed the oral language that enables the reading and writing on which we base most of our conceptions of achievement.

Once a child is labeled "learning disabled," it is very difficult to shed that identity, and, as Bart Simpson so poignantly observed, "Wait! We're supposed to catch up by going slower?" In fact, as students get older and are introduced to specialized terminology—denominator, predicate, reagent—those with more extensive vocabularies assimilate these words more easily, so, over time, the gap between high and low SES students grows ever wider.

Long story short, if we are serious about closing the achievement gap, it starts with introducing our kids to more words and supporting their use of those words so they can own them.

Language Use and Retention of Information

The *maximum* amount of time the human brain can absorb direct instruction—what we used to call lecture—is approximately twenty minutes. That is the time limit for the most motivated and mature brains, and, let's be frank, those brains are probably not in your classroom.

The rule of thumb for calculating the amount of direct instruction your students can handle is to take their age in years plus or minus three. So a typical third grader—eight years old—can absorb between five and eleven minutes of direct instruction at a time.

Limits of Working Memory

A number of explanations have been posited for why this is the case, but the one that makes the most sense to me involves the capacity of working memory (WM), which is where information is stored temporarily. In computer terms, WM is what is currently on the computer screen, whereas long term memory is in the hard drive.

It is generally understood that WM can hold approximately five to nine pieces of information at a time. If someone tells you their phone number, for example, you can remember those nine digits long enough to write the number down. If they add an international code, you may have to ask them to repeat themselves.

As we gain life experience and knowledge, we engage in what is known as "chunking," where those five to nine chunks contain more and more data. For example, someone first learning to read must sound out each phoneme. Thus, a five-letter word requires five chunks of working memory. As we grow in reading fluency, we store entire words in long term memory. Once students can recognize these words on sight, they will require only a single chunk of working memory, so the same amount of working memory is required to hold five words as used to be needed for only five letters. Over time, we become quite facile at reading very quickly, allowing us to combine unique combinations of words (sentences, paragraphs) into evermore data-rich chunks. We also have more and more schemata which allow us to assimilate these chunks of new information with things we already know and thus make meaning out of it all.

When we listen to a lecture, we engage in this same chunking process. The more we know about a topic, the longer we can take in new information about it. Eventually, though, the amount of new information exceeds the capacity of WM to assimilate it. Remember Lucy and Ethel in the chocolate factory? Like that.

Younger children and academically delayed students have fewer and less well-developed schemata, what E.D. Hirsch (1996) calls "intellectual capital." Now, I am not E.D. Hirsch's biggest fan, but just because he said something doesn't mean it's wrong. In the same way that those with large amounts of financial capital stand to make more money through investment, those with more background and contextual knowledge— intellectual capital—are capable of integrating more new information, more quickly.

Once the capacity of WM to integrate new information with old has reached its limits, there is very little benefit in continuing to supply new facts. Psychologists refer to a refractory period during which response to a second stimulus is slowed because the brain is still processing a previous stimulus. And, as with the more commonly recognized refractory period in the human body, continued stimulation yields little but frustration.

Several tell-tale signs indicate that your students' WMs have reached maximum capacity. Younger students will begin fidgeting uncontrollably. Older students' heads will tip to one side while their faces take on a blank, slack-jawed expression. During this period, what David Sousa (2011) calls "downtime," it is of immense benefit to students if teachers stop talking and set a task that requires students to process the information they have already been given.

The "Production Effect"

An additional concern in classrooms dominated by teacher talk is the reduced opportunity to leverage the "production effect" on memory. This is the phenomenon whereby students have memories not only of reading or hearing the material but also of producing the spoken representation of the material (McLeod, Gopie, Hourihan, Neary, & Ozubko, 2010).

In numerous experiments (Conway & Gathercole, 1987; Gathercole & Conway, 1988; Rivard & Straw, 2000), researchers have found that subjects who speak aloud what they are studying remember it with significantly greater accuracy than those who merely hear it, write it down, read it, or use a combination of those modalities.

Furthermore, when only selective material is vocalized, it becomes distinctive from everything that was not. Just as we remember better those individuals who distinguish themselves from the crowd—"You remember John? The one at the party with the stovepipe hat?" "Oh, right—John!"—we likewise remember academic material that is processed in a manner different from other material (Markman, 2010).

LANGUAGE USE AND WHAT IT MEANS TO TEACH

The word "educate" is derived from the Latin *educere*, meaning "to lead out." If we broaden our interpretation of that expression, it is not necessarily the children we are leading out but the capacity for understanding that already exists in each of them. When I *tell* my students things, I'm attempting to put information *in* their heads. Maybe it gets there; maybe it doesn't.

If, however, I create the circumstances under which they can tap their own intelligence to construct the information I want them to have and then tell me what it is, I have activated what is already there and *drawn it out* of them. Reinhart (200) (2000) arrived at the realization that a great teacher was not "one who explains things so well that students understand" but "one who gets students to explain things so well that they can be understood" (p. 478).

The benefits of this type of teaching are significant. When students tell us what they know, they also tell us what they don't know, allowing us to remediate deficits and misunderstandings quickly and efficiently. Furthermore, we remember the things we think about (Willingham, 2009). While teachers lecture, students can give the appearance of thinking without actually doing so. It is far more difficult to avoid thinking about a topic if you are discussing it or engaging in an inquiry about it.

CODA

Let us return to the Senior Composition classroom where we began and examine how that lesson might have played out if the teacher had been lucky enough to read this book first.

Our teacher explains nothing to her students, who are seated in pairs, but says instead, "You and your partner each have a different introductory paragraph. They're on different topics, different lengths, different tones, but they have something in common. Read your paragraph, compare it with your partner's, and see if you can figure out what that commonality is."

For a while, the room is silent as the students read. Eventually, selective students begin asking their partners, "What was yours about?"

"Dinosaurs. What about you?"

"Tornados."

"Hm. Well, that's not it."

Some pairs quickly get bogged down in picayune details like vocabulary or number of sentences. Others begin considering organization right away. The teacher allows these latter pairs to continue without her assistance. She intervenes with the former, but only when they appear to have reached an impasse, when they are unable to generate any new ideas.

"So we know it's not subject matter. What else do you have to think about when you're writing? What else do teachers grade you on?"

"Mechanics."

"Let's assume that both of these paragraphs are technically correct. What else?"

"Content."

"Which is kind of the same as subject matter."

"Um, organization."

"What's organization? How would you define it?"

"The way it's put together."

"Okay. See if there's anything similar about how these paragraphs are put together."

She then leaves them alone to continue their struggle and moves on to other pairs. She also checks in with pairs who believe they have identified the common thread.

"Whatya got?

"Okay, so, like, this one starts with a story, and you think you know the point that the story is going to make, but then the writer, like, says you're wrong and then he tells you, you know, what the right thing is."

"Okay, and what about the other one?"

"Um, that one starts with this quote that I think I saw it on a Snapple lid or something, like, it's really well-known, and, the writer, he says that nobody really understands what that quote is about, and then he makes this statement that backs up what he just said about everybody being wrong."

"Good. So what do they have in common?"

There's an extended pause.

"Um, there's what people think . . ."

"Uh-huh?"

"And then there's how they're wrong . . ."

"Keep going."

"And then what's actually the truth."

"Nicely phrased. Pair up with that other group—they have different paragraphs—and see if you all four can agree."

The teacher allows this process to go on until she feels confident that the students have teased out the basics of what she wants them to know. She then assembles the whole class and asks groups to volunteer their findings. She does not tell any single group they are correct but accepts all the offerings.

She then asks the class to evaluate whether the qualities offered by their peers are true across the board for each introductory paragraph. A few are rejected because they do not apply in some cases. Most are accepted.

Only at this point does our teacher provide her own terminology, which she and her students will use from here on.

"So most of you picked up on the fact that in the beginning the writer tells us something that you are either familiar with or agree with or just accept as a given. We call that 'establishing common ground.' Kyle, write that down."

Now, when Kyle writes this in his notes, he knows what it means.

"And then you saw that second part was when the writer said or implied that what we thought in the first part is wrong or not necessarily the case. That's the 'destablizing condition.'"

Kyle writes this unbidden.

"And finally the writer tells us 'this is what the deal is!' That is the thesis. Why don't we try writing one as a class and see how it goes?"

Some Thoughts Before We Begin

This concept attainment activity is not the only way to engage students with material and limit your own verbal contributions. In the following chapters, we will look at many more. I will also offer as much advice as I can to avoid the problems I have encountered during their implementation.

Everything here is presented with this caveat: You know your students better than I do. Use what works. Trash what doesn't. Change what you need to. And don't be afraid. No one went into teaching for the money. The only reason to stay in this profession is the continuous opportunity it offers to be creative and intellectually engaged and to allow our students to do the same.

CHAPTER 2

But my kids refuse to talk!

Many of you may already be convinced of the benefit of more student talk in your classroom. That's why you bought the book in first place. You've been trying to encourage more discussions, and your kids just aren't having it.

It is a source of eternal frustration to teachers that students who will not shut up when you need to tell them something will remain absolutely silent when you ask them to talk to each other. Reasons for this vary, but I address the most common below.

SOCIAL BARRIERS

In May of my first year of teaching, my students were discussing *Of Mice & Men*. One young man made an excellent point to which another student said, "I agree with the boy by the window..."

I was horrified. "The boy by the window?! That's Justin! You've been in class together for eight months! How do you not know *Justin*?"

A Difference Between Regular and Honors

I've heard more than a few teachers claim, "I can have discussions with my honors kids, but my regular kids just can't handle it." The assumption here is that honors students, by virtue of their superior intellect or work ethic, are more fitted to academic discourse than their less academically gifted peers.

I'd like to propose an alternative explanation. Honors students take honors classes, which tend to be smaller and fewer in number. As a result, honors students find themselves in many more classes with the same people over the course of several years. If the elementary and middle schools have a gifted program, it is possible for students to build a cohort that lasts twelve years. They may not like all their peers, but they know what to expect from them.

By contrast, so-called "regular" students may have a completely new set of peers every period of every day every year, giving them limited opportunity to build relationships. Consequently, they lack the trust that allows them to share ideas.

Cliques & Gangs

In addition, there are very real social castes that teachers ignore at their own peril. As they get older, student bodies balkanize according to a set of unwritten but ironclad rules that dictate where they can and cannot eat lunch, whom they can date, whose parties they can be invited to, what extracurricular groups they can join, and, most importantly, how enthusiastically they are allowed to contribute in class.

Unless a teacher has only students from a single social caste in his classroom, he will have to spend some time breaking down the barriers between students before they will collaborate successfully.

For several years, I taught a class for at-risk seniors. One year, two young men—one a Caucasian member of the football team, the other a Latino gang member—nearly came to blows several times during class, convinced that they were mortal enemies. I initiated a regimen of team building and class building exercises that would enable them to learn a little low-risk information about each other and discover some common ground. Eventually, they stumbled upon the fact that they both liked girls and getting high. I'll grant you, I may have created problems for authority figures elsewhere in the community, but, as far as my class was concerned, those two were no longer the source of any behavioral issues (and promised not to get high before or during my class).

If you want students who don't know each other to work collaboratively, you must first help them break down those social barricades. Assign them an activity that requires them to find out something about each other. For example, while you take attendance, ask each student in the group to speak for 30 seconds on any of the following topics, which are appropriate for students of any age:

- What did you do last weekend/what are your plans for this weekend?
- What's the coolest thing you've ever done?
- If you had $1,000,000 but only one day to spend it, what would you do?
- If you could talk to one of your relatives who is no longer here, who would it be and what would you talk about?

Clearly, this is not an exhaustive list. As you get to know your students better, you can provide topics tailored to their interests. In addition, there are a number of books with discussion prompts like the ones noted above. Titles that leap immediately to mind are *The Complete Book of Questions* (Poole, 2003), and *If. . . (Questions for the Game of Life* (McFarlane & Saywell, 2007).

There is no shortage of material out there. A Google search using the generic term "class building activities" yielded half a billion hits. On the other hand, not all of these activities are equally valuable or school-appropriate, and some require a significant amount of physical contact. I recommend staying away from those. A good rule of thumb is to ask yourself if you would want to participate in the activity with a stranger. If not, don't foist it onto your students.

Do some type of team building or class building activity three times a week—more if your students need it—and you will be amazed at the change that occurs in their willingness to participate and to support each other. I also recommend that you participate in these activities and share information about yourself. You are part of the team, and they need to know they can trust you as much as they trust each other.

LACK OF STRONG CONVERSATIONAL SKILLS

I learned the art of conversation at the dinner table and on long car trips. How to listen, ask questions, wait my turn—these are learned skills, but they are rendered unnecessary if the family doesn't eat together or are all engaged with personal electronic devices. Conversation as you and I may understand it does not happen in some students' homes.

The mistake teachers often make is assuming that, because their students cannot currently sustain a task-oriented conversation, they must be incapable of doing so. Anyone can learn to engage in academic discourse, but teachers must provide support while this skill is developing. Such support may take many forms:

Modeling

A former principal, Maria Ward, once said, "I'm not a big believer in 'do as I say, not as I do.'" She was referring specifically to teachers who don't allow students to have food or drinks in the room but keep a cup of coffee with them during class. I agree and try to extend that philosophy to other behaviors.

- How do you ask students to respond to your questions? Is it respectful and inviting or more like an interrogation?
- When students' answers are unclear, do you ask them to clarify or do you clarify for them?
- When they express opinions we find objectionable, do you disagree respectfully?

If we want students to engage in academic discourse, we have to do so as well.

Gradual Release

This term refers to the process of slowly handing over responsibility for engaging in the skill you are teaching through a combination of modeling and coaching:

I do. First, demonstrate the skill by yourself. Narrate your behavior as you do this, identifying each step and explaining what you're doing and why.

We do. Walk the class through the same process, calling on students to perform each step. You may need to perform several rounds of "we do" before you feel confident that students can do it on their own.

You (plural) do. Monitor small groups as they practice the process. Stop them early and often when you see behaviors you don't want or fail to see behaviors you do.

You (singular) do. When teaching academic conversation skills, this step would not be included, as discussion is a group task. If, on the other hand, you are teaching a solitary skill (writing an introductory paragraph, preparing a slide for the microscope, graphing polynomials, etc.), don't skip it.

Fishbowl Demonstrations

Place a group of students in the center of the classroom with other students seated in a circle around them. The group in the "fishbowl" need not have mastered the skill. They should, however, be students who are comfortable in the spotlight and can handle public constructive criticism. Have this group engage in the skill while the rest of the class watches and takes notes. Make sure you ask the larger group to notice what the fishbowl is doing right as well as where they can improve. At various points, stop the demonstration and ask the students in the audience for feedback.

Sentence Stems

Over time, "polite" society has developed a complement of verbal maneuvers designed to grease the conversational skids. They allow individuals to challenge each other while simultaneously indicating that offense is not intended. Provide your students with a variety of sentence starters that allow conversations to proceed respectfully but with academic rigor.

Adding more information.

- I agree with what _____ said about _____ and would like to add…

Disagreeing.

- While I respect the point ____ was making about ____, another way to look at it is…
- I hadn't considered _____'s perspective about _____. My thought was …
- I appreciate ____'s thoughts about _____. Can we also consider …?

It is essential that students first paraphrase the point that they are prepared to disagree with. Too often, people are listening not to understand but to know when it's their turn talk. Requiring students to paraphrase each other decreases this behavior.

Asking for clarification.

- Can you explain what you mean by…?
- I'd like to know more about …

Provide time for students to practice each of these maneuvers individually and repeatedly. Engaging in academic discourse is difficult and will not be mastered in a single class period. In my experience, even adults in graduate level courses tend to oversimplify each other's comments and shoot for a punchline over a thoughtful analysis. I encourage you to be patient and steadfast. The payoff if worth it.

The Discussion Topic is Too Broad or Too Narrow

When I was in elementary school, maybe second grade, our teacher asked us to write a story. We could write on any topic and it could be as long or as short as we thought necessary. I was paralyzed. Given complete freedom, I could not think of a single thing.

I was not alone, so the teacher revised the instructions: "Okay, um, write something about animals."

Bingo! A dozen ideas came to me. I settled on the origin of my guinea pig's name: Thursday.

A prompt that is too broad doesn't trigger anything in your students' memories, so they have nothing to say about it. By circumscribing the topic, you help your students zero in on what they know.

Likewise, some questions are too specific. Just because a question requires a detailed answer doesn't mean that it is likely to enable or encourage a discussion. If there is only one right answer, no matter how long, there is not much to discuss.

The difference between a strong conversation starter and a weak one can be a matter of degrees.

Subject	Too General	Slightly More Specific Question	Too Specific
English/ Language Arts	What did you think about the story?	How did the choices made by any of the main characters lead to their downfalls?	How did Max's decision to call the police lead to his downfall?
Art	How could this work be more dynamic?	How could the artist use any of the elements of design to create more movement?	How does the artist use lines to create movement?
Theater	How would you play this character?	How do the major characters' motivations change from Act I to Act II?	How did Stanley Kowalski's behavior affect Blanche?
Health	What should be done about childhood obesity?	How could we encourage children to be more physically active?	How much exercise should the average 4th grader get?
Math	How would you solve this problem?	Which of these three methods would you use and why?	When should you use the substitution method to solve an equation?
Science	Explain how adaptations help animals survive.	Consider a turtle, a giraffe, and a penguin. How do their differences help them survive?	How does a turtle's adaptations help it survive?

STUDENT SUFFERS FROM CHRONIC STRESS DISORDER

Much like soldiers with PTSD, students who have witnessed or been subjected to continual abuse, violence, or other extreme or ongoing forms of chaos, may develop coping skills that make group interactions very challenging (Jensen, 2009).

Students who are unable to turn off the fight or flight mechanism are always vigilant. In a discussion, they may interpret any disagreement with their ideas as a challenge and respond with verbal or physical aggression.

Students who are non-responsive play a perpetual game of possum, attempting to remain invisible and, therefore, safe. Anything they perceive as a threat will only create more stress and cause them to hunker down even further.

In either case, your first concern should be helping your students internalize the knowledge that your classroom is a sanctuary: emotionally, physically, and intellectually. You may have to slow down your plans to implement discussions and focus on building a sense of community in your room.

You should also consult with other professionals in your building: counselor, psychologist, social worker, etc. to see if the student requires legal or social services.

SUMMARY

Most students can learn how to have an academic conversation. Their current failure to do so is probably a function either of their social mores or their lack of previous exposure to academic discourse. Provide opportunities for students to get to know each other before asking them the work collaboratively. Then support their collaboration as you would any new skill: modeling, explicit instruction, and practice, practice, practice.

CHAPTER THREE

Think-Pair-Share

Early in their training, culinary students learn to make what are known as the five "mother" sauces: béchamel, velouté, espagnole, sauce tomat, and hollandaise. These sauces have few ingredients but require excellent technique for proper execution. The béchamel, for example, is a simple combination of fat, flour, and milk. Properly done, these ingredients form the creamy foundation of scalloped potatoes, New England clam chowder, lasagna, and macaroni and cheese. In unskilled hands, they are best used in papier maché.

Think-Pair-Share (TPS), also known as "turn and talk," is the mother sauce of classroom discourse. Deceptively simple, if done right it can improve memory and comprehension, engagement and critical thinking, as well as social skills, speaking and listening. Done wrong, it can lead to off-task behaviors, hostile interactions between students, and academic backsliding.

TPS is among the most versatile teaching tools you can have in your repertoire. I like it for several reasons:

1. **It requires almost no preparation.** Ideally, you would take some time during your planning to consider when in your instruction you should use it and what questions you should ask. But you can always fall back on the default question, "Take turns telling each other *anything* you remember about what I just said."

2. **Even my lowest performing students can successfully execute it.** Especially if you allow students to refer to their notes or the projection screen, it is the rare student who cannot meaningfully participate in some variation this activity.

3. **It ensures equal levels of participation.** When we tell students, "Turn to a neighbor and discuss _____," more often than not, one student will cover everything, and the other will nod. When students use a discussion protocol, even one as simple as TPS, they are forced to share the work.

4. **It raises the simultaneous active participation level in the classroom to 50%.** This not only increases engagement but lowers discipline problems. In a group of 20 children, each student represents a mere 5% of the class. When we ask students to *wait to be called on* under those conditions, we almost guarantee they won't be given the opportunity to contribute. Little wonder that students blurt out answers or tune out while others respond.

How it's Done

At its most basic, a TPS goes as follows:

Teacher: "Turn to your neighbor and take turns discussing what you've just learned."

Students do as asked.

Many of you may have tried this and found that your students sat and stared at each other. Alternatively, they chatted quite animatedly about many things, none of which applied to what they'd just learned.

A common teacher mistake is presuming that students know how to engage in academic discourse or even polite conversation. These are learned skills. In households where such conversations take place, children learn how to replicate them, and, because most teachers grew up in such households, they assume this skill is universal and innate. It is not, but it can be taught.

Step 1: Assign partners

You may be tempted to let this occur randomly or allow students to pick their own partners. Don't. In a battle between making smart choices and maintaining a social relationship, the relationship will almost always win. There are times when it may be appropriate to allow students to select their own partners, but this is not one of them.

Create pairs whose strengths buttress their partners' weaknesses. Strengths are not limited to academic achievement and can include such qualities as extroversion, kindness, curiosity, and popularity. Any of these characteristics, when properly leveraged, can lead a pair to become immensely productive, regardless of either students' grades or aptitude. Consider, for example, how a shy, serious student and a popular, struggling student might support each other.

Creating Pairs. The most effective method I have found for creating pairs is to write each student's name on an index card or sticky note. Under each name, write what that student's strengths are. Sometimes these can be hard to see, but adjust the deficit lens through which you may be viewing some of your kids and consider how behaviors you find irritating might work to those children's advantage with their peers. Do others view them as leaders, entertainers, protectors, spokespersons, etc.?

Create two equal rows of names. On the top row place the academically higher achieving students and randomly place another student's name under each. Now evaluate each pair.

- Do they have complementary strengths?
- Are they likely to work effectively together?
- Are they in the room at the same times every day, or do they frequently attend pull-out services at different times?

Switch the location of the bottom names until you find each pairing satisfactory. If you have an odd number of students in your class, create a trio that includes a student who is frequently absent.

Step 2: Create a workable seating arrangement.

In most of the classrooms I visit, at both the elementary and secondary level, the desks are arranged in clusters. The prevailing wisdom appears to be that collaborative groups are, axiomatically, superior to all other seating plans. I'm going to step out on a limb and assert that this is not *necessarily* true. Students who have poor self-monitoring skills find it difficult to focus on instruction in collaborative groups. This problem is compounded exponentially if their desks are positioned such that their profiles or, worse yet, their backs face the teacher.

For students still learning how to collaborate effectively, I recommend arranging your desks as follows:

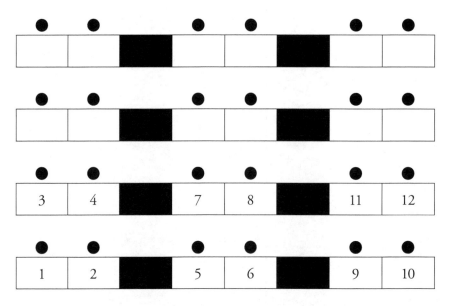

Students face the teacher but can quickly engage with a partner. In addition, there is no ambiguity about who each student's partner is; it is the person whose desk touches yours.

As students become more adept at collaboration and self-regulation, teachers can experiment with clusters. Students can quickly form such groups by having pairs of students on adjacent rows move their desks a quarter turn, as shown below:

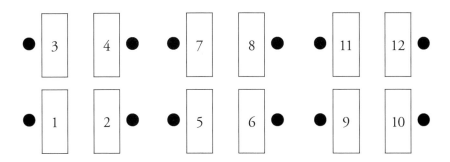

Step 3: Explicitly teach and model academic discourse and allow students to practice.

Ask a medium or low achieving student to serve as your partner for demonstration purposes. In doing so, you avoid the misperception that scholarly conversations are only for "brainy" kids or teacher's pets.

"Alice and I are going to take turns saying the names of movies we like for 15 seconds."

This may seem like a ridiculously short amount of time, but it is better for your students to run out of time before they run out of material than vice versa.

"Hold on while I set the timer so we'll know when to stop. Alice, take a few seconds to think of some movies, okay? And you go first."

Alice: Okay, *Zootopia*

Teacher: *Rocky*

Alice: *Harry Potter*

Teacher: *X-Men*

Alice: *Iron Man*

Teacher: *The Godfather*

Alice: *Lilo & Stitch*

Teacher: *Hook*

Alice: *Pocohontas*

Teacher: Ummmm

BEEP! BEEP! BEEP!

At this point, a lot of students are going to want to talk about one or more of the movies you mentioned or name their own favorites. Use this enthusiasm to your advantage.

"Does someone else want to try?"

Hands will shoot up. Select two people who have volunteered.

"Okay, you two are going to take turns doing the same thing while we watch. The person who goes first is the one who has the most letters on his shirt."

Allow these students to engage in this ping-ponging of ideas while the rest of the class observes. When the timer goes off, ask the rest of the class if they think they could do this. Most, if not all, will say yes.

"Great! I want to see it. I'm going to give you each a partner and you're going to try this while I walk around and see how you do."

Assign partners and have them sit facing each other.

"Now, the person who goes first is the person with the longer hair. Raise your hand if that's you."

Scan the room to make sure each pair has someone with a raised hand and that this person is, in fact, the one with the longer hair.

"This time, you're going to name snack foods. So think about all the stuff in the vending machine or on the chip aisle in the grocery store. Begin."

As students take turns listing items, circulate and make sure that they are 1) taking turns and 2) staying on topic. Praise them lavishly for doing so. Gently redirect those who are not.

It may require several practice sessions before all the partners are solidly on-task for the entire time. Do not allow this to frustrate you. Try staying physically close to pairs that seem more tempted than others to go off-task.

If you believe they have mastered the technique, you can now move them into using it to review content.

"That was awesome! We're going to do the same thing, only this time we're going to take turns telling each other something you remember about what I just taught you."

Ask a student to partner with you and, once again, demonstrate.

"So, we've been looking at the differences between viruses and bacteria. Jeremy and I are going to list as many as we can in 15 seconds. Jeremy, you start whenever you're ready."

"Okay. Bacteria have only one cell."

"Hmm, viruses are non-living things."

"Uh, some bacteria are good for you."

"Viruses are always bad for you."

"Oh, um viruses don't have a cell structure."

"Nice. How 'bout bacteria are smaller than viruses."

I don't…

Teacher: You can look at your notebook

BEEP! BEEP! BEEP!

VARIATIONS OF THINK-PAIR-SHARE

I call the interactions I profiled above "ping pong parlays." They are also known as rally robins. And they are the simplest form for students to master. As with any technology, however, the flatter the learning curve, the less flexibility it has. As students become more adept at academic discourse, you can set the timer for longer periods or have them engage in more complex versions of TPS that allow more nuanced conversations.

Timed Pair Share

Rather than taking turns, each student is given a certain amount of time to talk. When the timer goes off, Partner B picks up where Partner A left off. This is far more challenging than it sounds.

As I suggested earlier, set the timer for a shorter period of time than you think your students can converse. If they still have on-task things to say after both have contributed, you can let them take another turn, but you don't want them to run out of material before they run out of time.

If students do run out of material before their allotted time, their partners should ask them questions until the time is up. Otherwise, some students are apt to adopt as their default posture, "I don't know what to say," and then let their partner shoulder the burden of the entire discussion.

Think-Write-Pair Share

Ask a question or provide a prompt to students. Allow them a short amount of time (1-2 minutes) to write down their thoughts on the topic. Encourage them to use bullet points or whatever technique allows them to get as much information as possible on the page. When the designated time is up, each partner reads what she wrote.

I use this variation often, with adolescents as well as adults, for a number of reasons.

Reduces Stress: Some individuals experience great anxiety when asked to speak off-the-cuff, and among stress's many negative side effects is temporary memory loss. If you've ever run into an ex-lover while out with the current one and, when you attempted to introduce the two of them, couldn't remember the current one's name, you were experiencing stress-induced memory loss. With some responses committed to paper, a high-strung student is more likely to be able to participate meaningfully.

Enhances Memory. Half of remembering is the ability to get new information into long term storage. The other, often ignored, half is the ability to get it back out. When we hear an answer, we stop attempting to retrieve it from our own memories. This impedes the development of strong neural pathways that will allow us to access that information when we need it. Writing the answer allows everyone to practice retrieval.

Extends the thinking process: Depending on the topic, you can extend a think-write-pair share to propel students into more complex tasks or build upon their shared knowledge. Consider having them:

- take notes of interesting points their partners made;
- note how their responses differ;
- come up with more information that neither of them included in their original text.

Serves as an assessment/behavior monitoring device: If you wish, you can collect the writing. Much as we might like to think otherwise, some of our students may remain on-task only if they know *we* know they remained on-task.

Pair Share-Dictate

While Partner A speaks, Partner B writes what she says. Both partners must sign off on what the other has written to attest to its thoroughness and accuracy. This process can also be used not only for open-ended thought questions but also for something as comparatively simple as a worksheet or other written assignment.

For highly complex questions, teachers can limit the time each person speaks or writes. Some teachers have students work collaboratively on a small portion of the assignment, to practice in a supportive environment, and then complete another portion of it on their own as a means of assessing the understanding of individual students.

Make sure to scan the room frequently to make certain that the person speaking is not also the person writing, which defeats the purpose of the activity.

SUMMARY

Think-Pair-Share is the most basic form of student-to-student verbal interaction and, while it seems simple, it requires some planning for proper execution. Be thoughtful in creating pairs and seating arrangements. Likewise, be patient teaching each step of the technique to your students. Once they master the basics—taking turns, listening, staying on task— you can increase the complexity of their interactions by increasing the amount of time they converse or adding a written component to the discourse. Eventually, they will be ready for group conversations, which I cover in the next chapter.

CHAPTER 4

Discussion Protocols for Groups

Working in larger groups offers students the opportunity to hear and evaluate multiple points of view. When you feel confident in your students' ability to listen, take turns, and remain on-task in pairs, consider using these group protocols, which I have presented in what I believe is ascending order of complexity.

PAIRS PAIR

Task pairs with solving some sort of question or problem: mathematical, social, scientific or other. After conferring, have them join forces with another pair and share their findings. Or have Partner A explain to the other pair what Partner B said, and vice versa. Further challenge the foursome to come up with something new from their collaborative efforts.

ROUND ROBIN

Like the Ping Pong Parlay, a Round Robin asks students to state a single piece of information at a time. Let's assume, however, that you have taken the step of putting your students in a larger group because they are ready to have conversations that require more than a single byte of information at a time.

A very simple adaptation is to start by allowing each student to offer his single response. Then, when everyone has contributed an idea, the group can discuss their responses in greater depth.

Unfortunately, only the first student to speak is assured the opportunity of saying something original. Others may default to, "I was gonna say that," even if their response differed. My hope is that your students have overcome their fear of speaking their minds in front of each other by this time. However, it may be wise to have them first write their responses before anyone speaks, read them verbatim, and finally invite less structured sharing of ideas.

If you are concerned about one person hijacking the conversation, you might require that students stand while they are speaking. This encourages students to get to the point more quickly. It also allows you to manage behaviors from a distance. If you see someone who is speaking but not standing, someone who has been standing for an inordinately long time, or someone who has not stood yet, you can move toward that group to make sure the protocol is being followed.

PARAPHRASE & PRAISE

This technique is a useful bridge between a Round Robin and a more complex conversation like a Socratic seminar. The protocol requires active listening and specific feedback but provides scaffolding the help students build those habits.

Use Paraphrase & Praise with discussion questions that invite complex, open-ended responses. Mastery questions with limited variability in how to answer correctly will not allow students to respond with the variety necessary to enable the follow-up behaviors.

Sample Paraphrase & Praise Questions

	Weak Questions • Definite right and wrong answers • Limited variability in answers • No imagination required	Strong Questions • Multiple "correct" answers • Tremendous variability in answers • Speculation and imagination with evidentiary support required
ELA	What genre is this story and how do you know?	Pick a different genre and describe how the setting and the ending of the story would be different.
Science	Describe the steps in the hydro cycle?	How could you collect water at each stage of the hydro cycle?
Math	Talk through the process of solving for X.	There are three different ways to solve for X. Which would you use and why?
Social Studies	Explain the events that led to the American Civil War?	Was the American Civil War inevitable? What economic and political forces could (or could not) have prevented it?
FACS	What is the purpose of baking powder and how does it work?	You have a new bakery and want to turn a profit quickly. Taking into consideration cost, ease of use, and desirability of product, which levening agent (baking soda, baking powder, egg whites, or yeast) should you use and why?
Health	Identify the three macronutrients and explain the primary function of each.	Imagine you're a fitness trainer with a client who wants to lose ten pounds. He has high blood pressure. What specific diet recommendations do you make?

Steps

Discussion questions are written on individual cards. You should have at least as many questions as there are students in a group.

1. Person 1 draws a card from the pile and reads it aloud to Person 2.
2. After being allowed some think time, Person 2 answers in as much detail as possible.
3. Person 3 paraphrases the response using one of several paraphrase sentence stems, such as:
   - If I understand you correctly…
   - What I hear you saying…
   - Stop me if I'm wrong…
   - So, to sum up…
4. Person 4 praises the response using a praise sentence stem, such as:
   - Before you mentioned it, I never considered…I had always assumed…
   - I agree with you about …and would like to add…
   - I respect the point you made about…because….
5. Rotate roles and repeat Steps 1-4.

Prepping Your Students

Before turning this activity over to small groups, practice as a class. Draw a card and ask a random student to read the question aloud. Coach the student on reading slowly and clearly enough for others to understand what is asked.

Provide some wait time while everyone thinks of an answer. You might suggest that everyone write down a few thoughts before calling on anyone. Now, select another random student to answer the question.

Coach the student to answer in detail and at fairly great length. Such responses are desirable for several reasons. Extremely short answers need not be understood to be repeated. Lengthier answers require students to work on their listening and summarizing skills. Additionally, extremely short answers leave out essential details. Longer answers allow students to practice crafting well-supported responses. If they can talk through such an answer, they will have less difficulty writing one.

Select a third student at random and ask him to paraphrase the response. Direct students to the paraphrase sentence stems for their opening remark. Coach students to paraphrase accurately and completely. Check with the first respondent for accuracy. If a student cannot paraphrase her classmate's response, tell that person, "I'm coming right back to you, so pay attention" and ask another student to complete the paraphrase. Return to the first student and ask, "Can you please repeat what _____ just said?

Randomly select a fourth student and ask her to praise the response using one of the praise sentence stems. Coach students away from cop-out praises that give no meaningful feedback or indicate no thought has been given to either the initial response or the praise of that response, such as, "I agreed with the point you made about Hester Prynne because I thought that was a good point."

Repeat this process as many times as necessary to be convinced that your students understand how to execute each task properly.

Extensions

This protocol can be frustrating for the students who weren't asked the question but have ideas they want to share. As your students build proficiency in academic discourse, you'll want to include more viewpoints, particularly opposing viewpoints. Consider adding the following steps:

Open the floor. After Person 4 completes her praise, Person 1 can then invite others in the group to contribute. Provide them with invitation gambits:

- Does anyone else have something different to say?
- Are there any other contributions?
- I'd like to open the floor for other responses.
- Can anyone provide another perspective?

Anyone who has an alternative response to the question can answer, but disagreements must be preceded by a disagreement sentence starter and truncated paraphrase of the original response:

- While I respect what [student's name] had to say about [brief recap of first response] I'd like to suggest an alternative.
- In contrast to [student's name]'s view that [brief recap], I think _____.
- While I agree with [student's name] about _____, I'd like to focus instead on _____.

There is no limit to how many students can provide further responses but each must be preceded with a disagreement sentence starter and truncated paraphrase.

By placing these conditions on responders, you will lessen the temptation for students to speak simply because they enjoy the sound of their own voices. In addition, it is human nature to lash out when you feel devalued by someone else. You can reduce the number of arguments in your classroom if you ensure that students learn not only that two people who hold differing opinions can both be right but that there is a protocol for disagreeing while still showing respect.

Finally, the cockeyed idealist in me seeks to create a generation of citizens with the intellectual habit of knowing what they're disagreeing with before disagreeing. By requiring students to paraphrase each other's thoughts before offering their own, we interrupt the process whereby people listen only to know when it's their turn to talk.

Student-Supplied Questions. As your students develop more sophisticated questioning and answering skills, you may want to assign them the task of writing discussion questions for homework or as a Do Now activity. You'll probably need to do some explicit instruction on what makes a good discussion question. At minimum, questions should conform to the following criteria:

Text Dependent. The evidence for a thorough response must be found in the text being studied, not the students' personal experiences. While their experiences will necessarily inform their responses, most of the evidence must come from the material you have assigned. Consider the following two prompts for *Of Mice & Men*:

- If you were in George's place, what would you do?
- How does John Steinbeck want the reader to feel about Lenny's murder?

The first prompt requires no textual evidence to answer it completely. It uses the text only as a launch pad for student opinion. While there are times when you will want to solicit their opinions, my experience is that students are already expert at voicing them. What they lack is the ability to excavate text to find evidence in support of their opinions.

Multiple "correct" responses. If we reconsider the second question above, there are several supportable answers. Even if each student thought the murder was a necessary evil, multiple pieces of evidence exist to support that response:

- Candy's earlier assertion that he should have euthanized his own dog and not allowed someone else to do it for him;
- Curly's threat to shoot Lenny in the stomach so that he suffers before dying.

Conversely, a student can also support the idea that Steinbeck wishes the reader to feel a sense of hopelessness and futility:

- Lenny's history of accidental murders and assaults and the certainty that he would kill again in the future;
- The indifference with which Carlson and Curley regard the death of another human being and their puzzlement at Slim and George's melancholy over the event.

Begin by reviewing their self-generated questions to make certain they are 1) phrased clearly enough to be understood; 2) legible; 3) relevant; 4) school appropriate; and 5) text-dependent. Eventually, you may find that you can forego this step. Don't be discouraged, however, if that never happens. Kids are unpredictable. It's what makes teaching fun... and terrifying.

Socratic Seminars

The Socratic seminar is a formal discussion protocol in which students take full responsibility for asking questions, providing thoughtful responses, and reflecting critically on their own contributions. Although it is most often associated with high school classrooms, students of all ages can enact the seminar if they are taught how.

Many teachers I worked with raved about the success of their Socratic seminars, but when I observed, what I saw was underwhelming. For the most part, what teachers had been calling Socratic seminars were little more than informal discussions during which a small handful of students monopolized the speaking floor, expressing opinions unsupported by any textual evidence. Other students said little or nothing.

As I have written elsewhere in this text, we tend to take as axiomatic that a student-driven activity is superior to one that is teacher-led. I wish to go on the record with my objection to this assumption. Beyond the fact that poorly structured conversations allow students to fall into lazy habits of mind, I do not wish to contribute to the current crop of political and pop-culture figures who view facts as negotiable and believe the person who talks loudest is the one who should win the argument. I also return to Recurring Theme #1: Just because students are engaged does not necessarily mean they are learning.

The basic structure of a Socratic seminar involves a medium-large group (8-12 students) seated in a circle. Group members respond to thought-provoking, text-dependent questions, offering their own insights and interpretations; questioning, disagreeing with, or adding to each other's responses all in a respectful manner and citing textual evidence. The teacher's role is minimal, often limited to timekeeper. For a quick but thorough introduction to this technique, I recommend the video at the following link: https://www.teachingchannel.org/videos/bring-socratic-seminars-to-the-classroom

The more I observed, the more I came to believe that some students needed something to restrain their impulses and direct them toward more productive discussion while still maintaining majority ownership of it. While the ultimate goal is that students will self-monitor, I wanted to provide an external monitoring device that would support their growth in that direction.

Socratic Smackdown

I serendipitously stumbled upon this variation of the Socratic seminar at The Institute of Play's website. Socratic Smackdown rewards the behaviors you want to see, and penalizes those you don't, by assigning each of those behaviors a point value. Students gain or lose points based on how they engage with each other. I took the Institute's basic structure and tweaked it for my own purposes.

Students sit in two concentric circles. I find it useful to divide the class into thirds:

- Group A sits in the inner circle. These students engage in the discussion.
- Group B sits in the outer circle. Each student in Group B is assigned a student on the inner circle and keeps that student's score.
- Group C also sits in the outer circle. They are assigned a student from the inner circle and take notes on that student's contributions or missed opportunities.

In a class of 30 or so students, this distribution of labor keeps the number of students in the discussion manageable while providing meaningful work for those who are not actively taking part in the conversation. It also provides useful feedback to those in the inner circle without asking them to engage in reflection-in-action, which is immensely difficult.

Scorecards. This is the component that separates the Smackdown from the Seminar. Scorers keep track of behaviors demonstrated by those in the inner circle by placing tic marks on these cards. The content of the cards is dependent on what skills or behaviors you want to emphasize at that point in the year. When I first introduce the technique, I'm looking for students to 1) Ask good questions; 2) Support themselves with textual evidence; 3) Listen to each other; and 4) Take and yield the floor graciously. Therefore, my scorecard might look like this:

Skill	Pts	Tally Marks	Total
Asked relevant question	+2		
Provided textual evidence	+3		
Interrupted	-2		
Spoke extensively without providing evidence	-3		

Keep your scorecards simple by listing only the most important behaviors. As the school year progresses, some negative behaviors may be expunged and can be removed from the score card. Others may emerge and need to be remedied. Likewise, more basic conversational or analytical skills will be mastered, and you will want to incentivize students to attempt those with greater complexity. The score card might then look like this:

Skill	Pts	Tally Marks	Total
Added useful information to someone else's comment	+2		
Made relevant connection to text read earlier in the year	+3		
Spoke without adding any new insight or information	-3		

Ultimately, the goal is to eliminate the need for the score cards altogether. As with any tool, use it for as long as it supports your classroom goals. If you find that the scorecards are beginning to stifle rich discussion, toss 'em.

Timing. As with all student-to-student interactions early in the year, I set the timer for shorter periods than I think they can use. Remember Recurring Theme #2: Students should run out of time before they run out of material.

We start with a seven-minute round. After seven minutes, the students in the inner circle meet with their coach and their scorer for three minutes to find out how they're doing and what they could improve on.

We then return to the conversation for six minutes. Then roles rotate; Group A becomes the scorers, Group B becomes the coaches, and Group C moves to the inner circle. In a 90-minute block, all the students have time to serve in each role with time left over to complete their self-reflections.

As the year progresses and students become better versed in the art of discussion, you may find it useful to split the class in half instead of thirds. This will allow you to let discussions continue for longer periods and will prevent students in the outer circle from becoming bored, tasked as they are with serving as both scorer and coach.

Grading. I am often asked if I use the scorecards to grade the students' contributions to the discussion. In all honesty, I rarely look at the scorecards. Let's keep that between us. The value of those cards is not as an assessment tool but as a means of focusing my students' attention. That is not a rule, of course, and you should feel free to use the scorecards however they best serve your students' needs.

Some teachers make a big show of recording the scores of their first few seminars to encourage students to engage in the desirable behaviors. As those behaviors become habitual, teachers find less need to reward students for them.

Page Price, who is featured in the Teaching Channel video I recommended several pages ago, created quite a good rubric for assessing Socratic seminars. In Appendix 2, I have adapted her original document to allow you to track multiple students' contributions simultaneously. If you choose to, you can then transfer the information collected in Appendix 2 onto individual rubrics (Appendix 3) that you hand back to the students.

Final Thoughts on Group Discussions

Teachers, as a group, tend toward Type A personalities. As a result, any surrendering of control in the classroom can arouse anxiety. Their concerns typically boil down to one of two questions:

1. What if they don't hit the important points?

This is not a problem. Not only do students usually hit the important points, they often identify points that you missed. One of my solid C students identified a misconception I'd held through five readings of *Their Eyes Were Watching God*. If I had persisted in maintaining ownership of those discussions, I would still believe Teacake's story about throwing a party with Janie's money. Instead, this kid cited textual evidence that he was lying and lost her money in a dice game. Not only was I convinced by his argument, I contemplated having him evaluate every man who asked me out.

In the unlikely event that they miss an area on which you want them to focus, you can easily remedy that. Ask them a question that leads the group's discussions in the direction you need it to go. Alternatively, give a short lecture in which you highlight that point. You're still allowed to be an expert in your own classroom.

2. What if they don't say what I would say?

This is a problem, but only for the teacher. Your students may very well say things with which you disagree. Or they may agree but for different reasons. If they can do so respectfully and cite sufficient evidence to support their beliefs, this should make you ecstatic. It should also encourage you to reexamine your beliefs. We cannot expect students to be open-minded if we are not, likewise, willing to have our minds changed.

CHAPTER 5

Activities that Require No Talk

The impetus for teachers to talk less is to create "space" for students to think, reason, and interact. These behaviors do not require students to talk and can often be hindered when students speak prematurely.

I was a very eager participant in classroom discussions. Still am. And because I sound like I know what I'm talking about, others tend to defer to me. This is not necessarily a good thing for them or for me.

Quiet, introspective, or shy students may have great ideas that will never be heard if the only way they can share is verbally. At the same time, your more voluble students will not learn to listen and realize the value of others' opinions if they are rewarded for speaking early and often.

What follows are a few of my favorite activities that restrict or eliminate both teacher and student talk while encouraging creative and divergent thinking.

LIST-SORT-LABEL

This method of organizing information and ideas encourages students to make connections and think about topics in novel ways. Variations of this concept-mapping activity go by quite a few names.

In the 1960s, Japanese anthropologist Jiro Kawakita introduced the "affinity diagram" as a means of brainstorming solutions to the problems faced by Nepalese villagers. Hilda Taba (1971) included an activity called "List Group Label" in her *Teacher's Handbook to Elementary Social Studies*. More recently, an extension of the technique, "Generate Sort Connect Elaborate," appeared in Ritchhart, Church & Morrison's (2011) (2011) *Making Thinking Visible*.

Step One. List. Give a stack of sticky notes or pieces of scrap paper to each student in a group. Ask them to generate as many ideas as possible, placing only one idea on each piece of paper. For example, if I were introducing second graders to the idea of governmental services, I might ask them to list problems they see in their neighborhoods. Items on their sticky notes might include the following:

- Littering
- People not cleaning up after their dogs
- That crazy dude who hangs out on the corner
- Potholes
- Not enough sidewalks
- Graffiti
- The swings at the playground are broken
- The book I want at the library is always checked out

Students should complete this portion of the activity in silence. Allow listing to go on until you see students running out of new ideas.

Step Two. Sort. Group members work together to sort the slips of paper, placing together ideas or elements that are connected in some way.

Some connections may be obvious: "These all have to do with garbage." Some may be less so: "These problems are about the way things look," "These are about getting around."

Students may disagree on where an element belongs. Allow them to place that idea on a second slip of paper and sort it into both piles.

Some groups may have only two or three enormous categories. This typically happens when ideas are sorted into overly general categories. For example, when I ask young teachers to list and sort problematic student behaviors, some will place twenty or thirty slips of paper into a stack labeled "Verbal Behavior." I usually ask the group to dig a little deeper to determine what is at the heart of these behaviors. Eventually, they come around to smaller piles with such labels as "Trying to Get Attention" or "Resisting Authority."

Likewise, encourage students to look beyond such simplistic labels as "people," "events," "places," and the dreaded "miscellaneous." Ultimately, what goes into the piles is less important than the thought students give to how things are connected. Overly large piles suggest very little thought.

Although students should begin this portion silently, eventually it will become apparent that teams cannot make further progress without speaking. Allow them to converse at this point. They may struggle at this point as they are attempting to determine how a variety of disparate parts are related, but allow them to try, offer some guidance, and then leave them to try some more.

Step Three. Label. When groups are satisfied with their categories, they should create labels for each of them. Ideally, the labels have sufficient specificity to describe a meaningful relationship among the components and exclude most elements in other categories. It should not be so specific, however, that it cannot contain multiple elements.

Step Four (optional). Review. Allow students to circulate and review how other groups organized the information. Discuss these differences.

Why the Silence?

If you have been purposeful in your group formation, you have students with complementary skills sets: talkers with introverts, leaders with followers, etc. The silent rule allows quieter students' voices to carry weight equal to that of their more voluble peers. It further enables students who are unsure of the "rightness" of their responses to contribute without fear of ridicule.

What if they don't write anything?

Some students will either write nothing or wait until one of their peers writes something and then write the same thing. You may wish to implement a few failsafes to avoid such predicaments:

Practice with something easy. The first time you try List Sort Label, do it with a fun, non-academic topic such as movie titles or names of celebrities. Allow students to discover all the different ways a group of items can be categorized. Beyond their genres, for example, movies might land in such categories as 1) movies my parents would like, 2) date movies, 3) movies where the bad guy is British, 4) movies with at least one Baldwin brother, and so forth.

Assign the list portion for homework or individual seat work. This allows students to think without the pressure of doing so in front of others. It also enables you to make certain that everyone is pulling mostly equal weight. If you opt to review students' work before moving them on to the sorting step, you can also assess levels of understanding. I recommend the seat work option, as your lesson plan is apt to fall apart if a substantial portion of your students fail to complete their homework.

Adaptations

Teacher provides the listed elements. Give your students a stack of cards with information already written on them and ask them only to sort them into categories. Students who read or write very slowly will derive greater benefit from applying their mental energy to thinking about the items you provide than from creating those items.

Very young children can sort picture cards to demonstrate their understanding of shapes, food groups, animals, and the like. I have used this activity when introducing new vocabulary. Students sort the words based on how their definitions are related. In this way, they think about the words' meanings in a far less tedious manner than the more typical method of standing at the front of the room and reading each word and definition.

Teacher provides categories. Give students the category labels and let them create the elements, essentially turning the activity into a desk-sized graphic organizer. Don't tell them this. There is nothing inherently evil about graphic organizers, but, as the saying goes, familiarity breeds contempt. Sometimes, all that is necessary to excite students (and adults) is a little rebranding.

Dialogue Journals

This activity goes by other names. Depending on the context, it may be called silent argument, rally table, or tandem story. Students engage in a conversation of some sort but do so in writing, rather than verbally.

The teacher provides a prompt. It could be a quotation or question that is apt to elicit strong reactions. It might be the first sentence of a piece of fiction.

Students have a set amount of time to respond to the prompt. When the timer sounds, they trade papers with a partner. Each student now has a set amount of time to read what her partner wrote, consider its merits, and respond thoughtfully. This process continues until the teacher determines it has achieved it maximum level of effectiveness.

I find this technique especially helpful when dealing with topics that provoke emotional responses. Asking students to put their thoughts in writing accomplishes several things.

- It slows the response time, enabling students to consider the logic of their arguments before making them.
- It forces students to "hear" the arguments of those who may not share their views, preventing a thoughtful debate from degenerating into a shouting match where the loudest person can claim victory.

- Finally, it creates an archive of their thoughts, allowing all of us to reflect on the strengths or weaknesses of their arguments and how their thinking may change over time.

I have also used this technique in creative writing, albeit with mixed results. Students build a narrative by adding one sentence at a time. My colleague, Connie Cain, and I once passed a very enjoyable hour in this fashion during a faculty in-service.

This is not a technique to use if your goal is to create a strong, cohesive written product. It is, however, a great way to build esprit de corps. The story almost invariably collapses under the weight of its own ridiculousness, which can be great fun. Additionally, contributions can go south in a hurry. Below is an example of just such an incident that has been making the rounds on the Internet since 1997. I include it both as a cautionary tale as well as for its humorous properties:

> At first, Laurie couldn't decide which kind of tea she wanted. The chamomile, which used to be her favorite for lazy evenings at home, now reminded her too much of Carl, who once said, in happier times, that he liked chamomile. But she felt she must now, at all costs, keep her mind off Carl. His possessiveness was suffocating, and if she thought about him too much her asthma started acting up again. So chamomile was out of the question.
>
> Meanwhile, Advance Sergeant Carl Harris, leader of the attack squadron now in orbit over Skylon 4, had more important things to think about than the neuroses of an asthmatic, air-headed bimbo named Laurie with whom he had spent one sweaty night over a year ago. "A.S. Harris to Geostation 17," he said into his transgalactic communicator. "Polar orbit established. No sign of resistance so far . . ." But before he could sign off, a bluish particle beam flashed out of nowhere and blasted a hole

through the ship's cargo bay. The jolt from the direct hit sent him flying out of his seat and across the cockpit.

He bumped his head and died almost immediately, but not before he felt one last pang of regret for psychically brutalizing the one woman who had ever had feelings for him. Soon afterwards, Earth stopped its pointless hostilities towards the peaceful farmers of Skylon 4. "Congress Passes Law Permanently Abolishing War and Space Travel," Laurie read in her newspaper one morning. The news simultaneously excited her and bored her. She stared out the window, dreaming of her youth — when the days had passed unhurriedly and carefree, with no newspapers to read, no television to distract her from her sense of innocent wonder at all the beautiful things around her. "Why must one lose one's innocence to become a woman?" she pondered wistfully.

Little did she know, but she had less then ten seconds to live. Thousands of miles above the city, the Anu'udrian mothership launched the first of its lithium fusion missiles. The dim-witted wimpy peaceniks who pushed the Unilateral Aerospace Disarmament Treaty through Congress had left Earth a defenseless target for the hostile alien empires who were determined to destroy the human race. Within two hours after the passage of the treaty, the Anu'udrian ships were on course for Earth, carryingenough firepower to pulverize the entire planet. With no one to stop them, they swiftly initiated their diabolical plan. The lithium fusion missile entered the atmosphere unimpeded. The President, in his top-secret mobile submarine headquarters on the ocean floor off the coast of Guam, felt the inconceivably massive explosion which vaporized Laurie and 85 million other Americans. The President slammed his fist on the conference table:

"We can't allow this! I'm going to veto that treaty! Let's blow 'em out of the sky!"

This is absurd. I refuse to continue this mockery of literature. My writing partner is a violent, chauvinistic, semi-literate adolescent.

Yeah? Well, you're a self-centered tedious neurotic whose attempts at writing are the literary equivalent of Valium.

You total $#!

Stupid %!+©#

As amusing as this interchange is, it illustrates the necessity of continuous monitoring of student interactions and of timely interventions when the rules of civility are threatened.

DEBATE TEAM CAROUSEL

This protocol is adapted from Himmele and Himmele's (2011) *Total Participation Techniques*. It supports students as they learn to engage in written argumentation while simultaneously reducing tedium and requiring students to assume multiple points of view.

Each step of this activity can be altered to suit your students' level of advancement or the specific skills you are focusing on. For instance, according to the Common Core State Standards, opinion writing at the third-grade level requires students to do the following:

- Introduce the topic, state an opinion, and create an organizational structure that lists reasons;
- Provide reasons that support the opinion;
- Use transitional words and phrases to connect opinion and reasons; and
- Provide a concluding statement or section.

To use the Debate Team Carousel with third graders, the teacher would have students read and make notes on one or more pieces of text. In groups of four, each student begins an argumentative paragraph by stating an opinion about the reading. Students place their initials after their contribution and then rotate their papers clockwise (or counterclockwise— as long as everyone passes in the same direction).

Students read the claim provided in the previous step and then search out a reason in the text that supports this opinion. They write a sentence using a transitional word or phrase to connect the reason to the opinion stated in step one. Again, they initial their work and rotate the papers.

Students read what their two colleagues have written so far. They then provide a second piece of textual evidence to support the original claim. They initial and rotate papers a third time.

Finally, students offer a concluding sentence.

Teachers can modify this activity to suit older or more advanced students by changing the tasks required at each step. Appendix 6 includes sample worksheets that represent opinion writing standards at two different levels.

CHAPTER 6

Sample Lessons with Minimal Teacher Talk

The key to raising both engagement and rigor while necessitating less teacher talk is to intentionally omit information and require that students figure out what that information is. When designing an activity, first determine what it is you wish students to see. Now ask yourself, "How can I remove the thing that I want them to see, whereby its very absence will make it more visible?"

If I want students to understand the function of verbs, I will provide them with sentences that are missing the verbs and ask them what the problem is. If I want students to recognize how the exponent affects the shape of a curve, I will give them multiple examples and ask them to identify a trend.

The reason this works is pretty simple: people like puzzles. We devour mystery novels and sudokus and shows like *The First 48*. We enjoy figuring things out. What greater pleasure can there be than identifying the killer's motive before Detectives Goren and Eames do?

If we frame our content as a mystery to be solved, rather than as a foregone conclusion arrived at by someone else who did all the thinking for them, our students have a reason to engage. This is true at all grade levels and in all areas of study.

The examples that follow are intended to demonstrate the general framework of lessons with student talk and reasoning at the center. The better you know your content and your students, the more creative you can be in your lesson design, but you should also feel free to use these examples as templates.

IDENTIFYING DISTINGUISHING CHARACTERISTICS

By the end of kindergarten, students should be able to "correctly name shapes, regardless of their orientation or overall size" (Common Core State Standards Initiative, 2017). Today, I want to introduce my students to the triangle.

Assemble sufficient examples: Make sure there are different sizes and colors, solid triangles and triangles with hollow interiors, scalene, isosceles, and equilateral triangles. You'll want to cherry-pick these examples. In later class periods, you can show students triangles formed in other structures, such as the eaves of a house or by the diagonal beam across a barn door. There will likely be other shapes in such a photograph that may make the task too challenging or lead them to form misconceptions that are very difficult to expunge.

Facilitate the investigation. Give each of your students a triangle and let them trace it with their fingers or pencils. Ask them to think about what makes it special or interesting. Now pair students and have them compare their triangles using one of the conversation protocols laid out in Chapter 3. Allow them to continue until either a) they run out of things to say or b) an amount of time determined by the teacher elapses.

While the goal is for students to determine what is the same about both of their shapes, at this point, the sample is too small to eliminate extraneous variables such as size or color. Once the pair has decided what their shapes have in common, shuffle the pairs and have them repeat the process. Do this a few more times until you feel confident that a critical mass of students has correctly identified the common elements.

Encourage students to use their own vernacular. Part of why this method is useful is that students form working definitions of new concepts using words that make sense to them. This is a far more natural and effective way to build a vocabulary—letting the concept precede its label—than what we so often do: providing the label first.

As your students work to compare their shapes, they may describe their commonalities in ways that only five-year olds can:

- They're both straight but bendy in the straight parts
- There's three of them.
- It's pointy in three places.

All that matters is that the observations are accurate and make sense to the students.

Collate the data. Pull the class together and allow volunteers to tell the rest of the class what their shapes had in common. List what each says on the board. When all the groups have had an opportunity to share, remind the class, "Remember, we are looking for something that ALL of our shapes have in common. So if even one of our shapes doesn't have this characteristic, we have to find something else."

Now have your students test each hypothesis against the data. The only things that all the shapes have in common are their three sides/angles.

At this point, you can give them the vocabulary terms TRIANGLE, SIDE, and ANGLE. You can even build some recognition of Latin prefixes by asking if students know the Spanish word for three (*tres*). Ask them why this shape would be called a TRI-ANGLE.

Assess the understanding. Give pairs or groups of students a stack of cards with an assortment of shapes on them. Ask them to sort their cards into two categories: Triangles and Not Triangles. Finally, give individual students a worksheet with various shapes on it. Have them draw a smiley face next to each triangle and a frowny face next to any other shape.

Extension. Ask students to find triangles within the classroom. Point out a few examples, both easy and difficult to find, such as the negative space formed when a book leans against the side of a bookcase or the picture on the front of a bag of tortilla chips.

Generalizing to other grades and subject matter

Zero in on the characteristic you want to highlight and cherry-pick simple, perfect examples of it. These examples can be graphic images, short pieces of writing, video or audio clips. Just be certain that the characteristic you want students to identify is present and unobscured in each. Give students time to compare the examples, compare notes with each other, formulate and test inchoate hypotheses. Pool the class's ideas and reach agreement on what the common thread is, letting the students articulate that distinguishing characteristic in their own words. Finally, provide them with the subject-specific vocabulary for this characteristic.

UNDERSTANDING THE BASICS OF A SYSTEM OR PROCESS

By the end of third grade, students should "understand human body systems and how they are essential for life: protection, movement and support" (NC Department of Public Instruction, 2017).

Create an Analogy. Most manmade systems and processes are analogous to, if not modeled after, those existing in nature. If we want our students to have a basic understanding of what happens at each stage in the system or process, we simply need to find an analog with which our students are familiar and have them analyze the component parts.

As far as third grade science is concerned, the components that protect, support and move the human body are the muscles, bones, and skin. Children tend not to struggle with the role of bones and muscles, but the idea of skin as a means of protection can elude some children.

A useful analog is a small tent, the kind you might use on a camping trip. If possible, set up a tent in your classroom. If not, provide students with exterior and interior photographs of it and ask them to discuss and analyze the function of each part. They will quickly recognize that the poles offer structure while the canvas protects whatever is inside.

Assess the Understanding. Now ask them to write for a few minutes on the following prompt: "How is your body like a tent?" At this age, they should be able to call upon vocabulary like *bones* and *skin*. They may add other observations, based on previous learning: the canvas keeps out mosquitoes like the skin keeps out germs. As they become more confident with their analogies, you can provide them with the terms *skeletal system* and *integumentary system*. You could even place those labels on the tent to further concretize the concept.

Warning. This can be a very powerful technique, but it comes with some risk. Because any analog is imperfect in its similarity to the thing you want your students to understand, you may unintentionally generate misunderstanding. For example, unlike the structure of the human body, the "bones" in a tent come in direct contact with the "skin."

Doug Lemov (2010) recommends that teachers "excavate errors." If you suspect that a particular lesson will yield student misconceptions, go looking for those misconceptions early. Ask questions that intentionally reveal inaccurate thinking.

PRESENTING A LOT OF FACTS

According to the social studies standards in my current state of residence, by the end of eighth grade, students should be able to explain "how changes [in transportation, communication networks and business practices] affected individuals and groups" and "how human and environmental interaction affected quality of life and settlement patterns" (NC Department of Public Instruction, 2017)

Assemble the Facts: At each cluster of tables, I place a selection of documents. There are a variety of maps, each highlighting a different feature: highways, airports, seaports, topography, exports, and major industries. There are graphs and charts that feature such information as income, education, home prices, weather, etc. There are also very short articles (2-3 paragraphs) that reveal information about various places around the state.

Facilitate the investigation. Groups of students will study the documents and discuss their content in light of this question: If Blackbeard were alive and well and living in North Carolina today, where would he place his hideout and why? Blackbeard is part of the state's history and a perennial fascination to old and young alike. By asking students to place him in a modern context, I am also asking students to consider many complex factors:

- What is considered "treasure" today? Where would you find it?
- Is it of greater benefit to live somewhere remote or somewhere with well-developed infrastructure?
- How do conflicting needs for safety, opportunity, excitement, status, etc. affect the desirability of a location?

Provide students with a graphic organizer that helps them view both the pros and cons suggested by each document. If necessary, give them a protocol with which to discuss the content of the documents. One of my favorites is See-Think-Wonder (Ritchhart, Church, & Morrison, 2011).

See-Think-Wonder. Students first list observations: What is objectively present in the document? Next, they make interpretations based on their observations: Given that _____ is present, what do I think it means? For example, I see that the Charlotte area has a large number of banks. I think that means there's a lot of rich people living in or near Charlotte. Finally, they ask questions prompted by their observations and analyses: I wonder if it would be smart to have the hideout there so the pirates could rob banks and rich people, instead of ships like in the old days.

Give groups time to examine each set of documents, discuss their findings and update their hypotheses regarding the fitness of various locations. Remember, the answer at which they arrive is less important than the thinking that goes into it.

Assess the understanding. Assign each student to write a persuasive paragraph in which she defends the appropriateness of a single location by citing evidence of transportation, industry, natural resources, and any other relevant data contained in the documents they reviewed. I prefer to assign individual essays at this point for a few reasons:

- My quirkier or highly gifted students may have fascinating ideas that are too complex or too weird for their group members to appreciate. I don't want to squelch their thinking or creativity.
- Group writing assignments do not provide the learning data I need. While I am a huge fan of *learning* as a cooperative activity, I do not care for cooperative *assessing*. At the end of the day, I need to know just how much each of my students does or does not understand.

Generalizing to other subject matter

In his delightful book *Why Don't Students Like School?,* Dan Willingham (2009) explains that the facts we want students to remember—the Pythagorean theorem, the atomic number of carbon, the names of the original thirteen colonies—are all partial answers to a larger question. The answers alone are not very interesting, but the question usually is. Unfortunately, we often get so caught up in providing students the answers that we forget to ask the right questions, what McTighe and Wiggins (2013) call essential questions.

When faced with a great many pieces of information you want your students to know, ask yourself a very difficult question: Why would anyone need to know this? Helpful hint—the answer is never *because it's on the test.* Theoretically, it's on the test because it's necessary. What makes this information useful or necessary to someone who believes it is both those things?

Consider the sort of questions that practitioners in the field ask themselves:

- How can I use what I know to predict what will happen in the future?

- How can I fix this problem?
- How can I communicate most effectively with this particular audience?

These questions underpin all four core disciplines: math, science, social studies and English/language arts. Something as simple as arithmetic allows us to predict if we have enough money to last from one paycheck to the next. How much more compelling would mathematics instruction be if we convinced our students we were imbuing them with clairvoyant powers?

CREATING SCHEMATA

The set-up for this technique does not differ significantly from that for presenting a great many facts. The goal, however, changes. You do not need them to arrive at a conclusion; you are simply trying to tickle their interest and, ideally, their compassion so that they can visualize and empathize with the characters about whom they will be reading.

Most literary "classics" seem quite remote to our students. Although their themes may be timeless, everything else is rooted firmly in the time and place of the novel's setting, and students will struggle to comprehend the book's meaning without some type of anticipatory set. Many teachers rely on the K-W-L –What do you **K**now? What do you want to **W**ant to know? What have you **L**earned?—to activate prior knowledge.

My experience with K-W-L charts was almost uniformly disappointing. Often my students were fiercely proud to know nothing about the topic and demonstrated an equally fervent lack of desire to learn anything about it. Alternatively, they thought they knew a lot about it, but almost all of it was incorrect. When no schema exists, our job shifts from activating to generating prior knowledge.

Assemble the Data. Let's say you're beginning a unit on *The Grapes of Wrath*. Determine what concepts are most necessary to the understanding of the novel. Present these concepts in as graphic a form as possible:

photographs, video clips, mp3 files, newspaper articles, journal entries, and other relevant media. As much as possible, look for items that humanize the obstacles and conflicts in the novel. Collating such artifacts is made fairly simple by the existence of Google and even simpler by such online resources as The *American Experience* (http://www.pbs.org/wgbh/americanexperience/) and OER Commons (www.oercommons.org).

Organize the data in categories: Dust Bowl, Great Depression, labor movement, westward migration, 1920s automobiles, etc. Take some time to consider what *your* students specifically might not know. City kids, for example, might not have any concept of how farming works, making the entire first chapter a complete mystery. A single aerial photograph of drought-stricken farmland will provide a mental model that will allow Steinbeck's words to make sense.

Facilitate the investigation. You may have noticed that I'm expending much less effort than I did earlier in the book on how to get kids to talk about content. My hope is that, as your year progresses and your students form habits of discourse, you will also have to exert less control over their conversations. This leaves you more time to do the more interesting work of crafting activities that enable their thinking.

If, however, your students have not yet internalized your conversational expectations, you can use any of the protocols from Chapter 5 or See-Think-Wonder (above). Now is also a great time for a graffiti walk.

Graffiti Walk. Armed with a stack of sticky notes, students approach an artifact. This can be done alone, in pairs or in groups. They discuss what they see and write a response, either directly to the artifacts or to a comment left by a previous group. You can set some parameters on what they write. For example, you might ask them to focus on what the conditions presented in the artifact might cause a person to do or feel. Once students have examined each artifact, allow them to walk through the collection and read what others have written.

Assess the understanding. Ask students to formulate several predictions about the content and possibly the themes of the novel, justifying their responses by citing two or more of the artifacts they viewed. This can be done in writing, although I prefer a discussion if I'm simply introducing and building interest in a new topic. When they refer to specific groups of artifacts, you can offer specialized vocabulary they may require to successfully navigate the unit.

SUMMARY

We can raise engagement and still "cover" the curriculum if we present the material as a mystery to be solved. If students are asked to recognize patterns, deconstruct analogies, or answer an essential question, they cannot avoid engaging with the material. When they engage with the material, they cannot avoid understanding it. The teacher's responsibility changes from dispenser of information to facilitator of inquiry. We don't provide answers; we ask good questions and then guide students to construct the answers themselves.

How to select who goes first

Not all of these are appropriate for all students. Know your kids and use the ones that work for them. Ignore the ones that don't. Make up your own and let me know about them. I'll add your contributions to later editions of this book.

GO FIRST IF YOU...

1. Have the longest (or shortest) hair
2. Have the largest (or smallest) hands
3. Have the most pockets on your outfit
4. Have the most letters on your shirt
5. Have the birthday closest to today/Christmas/St. Patrick's Day/etc.
6. Have eaten a burrito/pizza/burger/etc. most recently
7. Are the tallest
8. Bench press the most
9. Run the fastest 40-yard dash
10. Have run the longest distance at one time
11. Have the most freckles on your nose
12. Can sing the highest note
13. Play the most different musical instruments
14. Can recite pi to the greatest digit
15. Have the most siblings (biological and step)
16. Have traveled the farthest from home
17. Live closest to school
18. Ride the longest time on the school bus
19. Are taking the most AP courses
20. Have the most followers on Facebook/Twitter/Instagram/etc.
21. Got the most likes on your most recent post
22. Have the most letters in your last name
23. Have the most pets
24. Have the most allergies
25. Are wearing the most jewelry
26. Have the longest nails
27. Have the cleanest sneakers
28. Have the oldest grandma
29. Have the most visible piercings
30. Have the youngest sibling

OTHER OPTIONS

31. Have students play a quick round of Rock-Paper-Scissors
32. Have students rate on a scale of 1-100 their interest in/desire for/loathing of/etc. something. For example, "How prepared do you feel for the test on Friday?" Have them write their answers secretly on a piece of scrap paper. Simultaneously, reveal responses. Larger (or smaller) number goes first.

Socratic Seminar Checklist

(Adapted from "Socratic Seminar: Patience & Practice" at https://www.teachingchannel.org/videos/bring-socratic-seminars-to-the-classroom)

	Name	Name	Name	Name	Name	Name
Proficient: Does all of the following						
Comes to discussion prepared						
Uses body language and eye contact to indicate active listening for the duration of the seminar						
Both asks and answers questions						
Participates by doing at least one of the following:						
Building on the thoughts of others						
Asking clarifying questions						
Quoting the text to support a point						
Using language of recognition and appreciation to promote collaboration and collegiality						
Advanced: Proficient + at least two of the following						
Actively incorporates others into discussion						
Challenges ideas and conclusions						
Summarizes points						
Qualifies or justifies own views						
Makes new connections based on new evidence or reasoning presented by others						

Basic: Student meets 2-3 of the *proficient* criteria

Below Basic: Student meets only 1 of the *proficient* criteria

Far Below Basic: Student meets none of the *proficient* criteria

Socratic Seminar Rubric

(Adapted from "Socratic Seminar: Patience & Practice" at https://www.teachingchannel.org/videos/bring-socratic-seminars-to-the-classroom)

Name:_____

Standard Addressed

o SL.9-10.1. Initiate and participate effectively in a range of collaborative discussions (one-on-one, in groups, and teacher-led) with diverse partners on grades 9–10 topics, texts, and issues, building on others' ideas and expressing their own clearly and persuasively.

o Come to discussions prepared having read and researched material under study; explicitly draw on that preparation by referring to evidence from texts and other research on the topic or issue to stimulate a thoughtful, well-reasoned exchange of ideas.

o Work with peers to set rules for collegial discussions and decision-making (e.g., informal consensus, taking votes on key issues, presentation of alternate views), clear goals and deadlines, and individual roles as needed.

o Propel conversations by posing and responding to questions that relate the current discussion to broader themes or larger ideas; actively incorporate others into the discussion; and clarify, verify, or challenge ideas and conclusions.

o Respond thoughtfully to diverse perspectives, summarize points of agreement and disagreement, and, when warranted, qualify or justify their own views and understanding and make new connections in light of the evidence and reasoning presented.

Advanced: Student meets *all* of the *proficient* criteria plus *two or more* of the following:

☐ **Actively incorporates** others into the discussion

☐ **Challenges** ideas and conclusions in thoughtful, well-reasoned exchange of ideas

☐ **Summarizes** points of agreement and disagreement

☐ **Qualifies** or **justifies** own views and understanding

☐ **Makes new connections** in light of the evidence and reasoning presented

Proficient

☐ Student comes to discussion **prepared** (with **completed preparation notes and text**)

☐ Uses **body language** and **eye contact** to indicate **active listening** for the **duration of the seminar**

☐ Both **poses** and **responds** to **questions**

☐ Participates by doing at least one of the following:

　　o **Building** on the thoughts of others by using appropriate transition words and phrases

　　o Asking **clarifying** questions

　　o **Quoting** the text to support a point

　　o Using language of **recognition** and **appreciation** to promote **collaborative, collegial discussions**

Basic: Student meets 2-3 of the *proficient* criteria

Below Basic: Student meets only 1 of the *proficient* criteria

Far Below Basic: Student meets none of the *proficient* criteria

Socratic Smackdown Scorecard
and Coaching Notes

Name of Person in Inside Circle: _____

Name of Coach: _____

Behavior	# pts	Tally for each occurrence	Subtotal
Asks for clarification of point made by another	+1		
Summarizes another speaker	+2		
Uses text to support response	+2		
Asks thoughtful follow-up question of a participant	+3		
Interrupts another speaker	-1		
Digresses unproductively	-3		

Coaching Notes and CONFERENCE!

1. A great point you made during Round I was:

2. A great behavior you showed during Round I was:

3. A missed opportunity (behavior or discussion point) during Round I that I noticed was:

4. A goal for our team during Round II is:

Two "glow" comments for this participant:

A "grow" comment for this participant:

APPENDIX 5

Coach's Reflection

On a scale of 1-5, 1 being "not at all" and 5 being "exceptional," rate...

1. ...how well your coach/inner-circle collaboration worked.

        1   2   3   4   5

Cite *specific evidence* to explain the above rating.

2. ...how well you fulfilled your role as a coach.

        1   2   3   4   5

Cite *specific evidence* to justify the above rating.

Finally, reflect upon the discussion as a whole. What issues do you wish had come up? What points would you have brought up? What would you do differently if you were to coach again?

APPENDIX 6

Inner Circle Reflection

On a scale of 1-5, 1 being "not at all" and 5 being "exceptional," rate...

1. ...how well your coach/inner-circle collaboration worked.

1   2   3   4   5

Cite *specific evidence* to justify this rating.

2. ...how well you fulfilled your role as a participant in the discussion.

1   2   3   4   5

Cite *specific evidence* to justify this rating.

Finally, reflect upon the discussion as a whole. What would you do differently if you had the opportunity? If you were in the coaching role, what advice would you give yourself?

Sample Debate Team Carousel Worksheets

Six Grade Opinion Writing	
1. State a claim about the topic addressed in the reading.	2. Find the most important or strongest piece of evidence to support the claim made in step one. Write one or more sentences that include the evidence and use words that let the reader know that this is the strongest evidence (e.g. most importantly, first and foremost, above all, etc.)
3. Repeat step two with the second strongest piece of evidence you can find.	4. Write a concluding sentence that sums up the argument.

9-10 Grade Opinion Writing	
1. Make a claim about the topic addressed in the reading. Introduce not only your opinion but establish why this issue is important.	2. Provide evidence for this claim by embedding a relevant direct quotation, formatting and citing it correctly, and explaining its relevance to the claim. Use appropriate transitions.
3. Make a counterclaim and provide evidence to support it. Use an appropriate transitional word or phrase.	4. Write a concluding sentence that resolves the argument.

Works Cited

Common Core State Standards Initiative. (2017, June 29). *Kindergarten>>Geometry*. Retrieved from http://www.corestandards.org/Math/Content/K/G/

Conway, M., & Gathercole, S. (1987). Modality and long-term memory. *Journal of Memory & Language, 26*(3), 341-361.

Csikszentmihaly, M. (1990). *Flow: The Psychology of Optimal Experience*. New York: HarperCollins.

Darn, S. (2007). *Teacher Talk Time*. Retrieved from https://www.teachingenglish.org.uk/article/teacher-talking-time

Fisher, D., Frey, N., & Rothenberg, C. (2008). *Content-Area Conversations: How to Plan Discussion-Based Lessons for Diverse Language Learners*. Alexandria, VA: Association for Supervision and Curriculum Developent.

Gathercole, S., & Conway, M. (1988). Exploring long-term modality effects: Vocalization leads to best retention. *Memory & Cognition, 16*(2), 110-119.

Hart, B., & Risley, T. (2003). The Early Catastophe. *American Educator*, 4-9.

Hirsch, E. (1996). *The Schools We Need and Why We Don't Have Them*. New York: Random House.

Jensen, E. (2009). *Teaching with Poverty in Mind: What Being Poor Does to Kids' Brains and what Schools Can Do About it*. Alexandria, VA: Association of Supervision and Curriculum Development.

Kounin, J. S. (1970). *Disciplie and group management in classrooms*. Holt Rinehart Winston of Canada.

Lemov, D. (2010). *Teach Like a Champion 2.0: 62 Techniques that Put Students on the Path to College*. San Francisco: Jossey-Bass.

Markman, A. (2010, May 11). *Say it loud: I'm creating a distinctive memory*. Retrieved from https://www.psychologytoday.com/blog/ulterior-motives/201005/say-it-loud-i-m-creating-distinctive-memory

McFarlane, E., & Saywell, J. (2007). *If...(Questions for the Game of Life)*. New York: Villard.

McLeod, C., Gopie, N., Hourihan, K., Neary, K., & Ozubko, J. (2010). The production effect: Delineation of a phenomenon. *Journal of Experimental Psychology, Learning, Memory and Cognition, 6*(3), 671-685.

McTighe, J., & Wiggins, G. (2013). *Essential Questions: Opening Doors to Student Understanding*. Alexandria, vA: Association for Supervision and Curriculum Development.

NC Department of Public Instruction. (2017, June 30). *Essential Standards: Fourth Grade Social Studies*. Retrieved from K-12 Standards: Curriculum and Instruction: http://www.dpi.state.nc.us/docs/curriculum/socialstudies/scos/unpacking/4th.pdf

Poole, G. (2003). *The Complete Book of Questions: 1001 Conversation Starters for Any Occasion*. Grand Rapids, MI: Willow Creek Association.

Reinhart, S. (2000). Never say anything a kid can say! *Mathematics teaching in the middle school, 5*(8), 478-483.

Ritchhart, R., Church, M., & Morrison, K. (2011). *Making Thinking Visible: How to Promote Engagement, Understanding, and Independence for All Learners.* San Francisco: Jossey-Bass.

Rivard, L., & Straw, S. (2000). The effect of talk and writing on learning science: An exploratory study. *Science Education, 84*(5), 566-593.

Sousa, D. (2011). *How the Brain Learns.* Thousand Oaks, CA: Corwin.

Taba, H., Durkin, M., Fraenkel, J., & McNaughton, A. (1971). *A Teacher's Handook to Elementary Social Studies: An Inductive Approach.* Reading, MA: Addison-Wesley.

Weimer, M. (2012, June 20). *Magna Publications.* Retrieved from Faculty Focus: https://www.facultyfocus.com/articles/teaching-professor-blog/five-reasons-getting-students-to-talk-is-worth-the-effort/

Willingham, D. (2009). *Why don't students like school?* San Francisco: Jossey-Bass.

Made in the USA
San Bernardino, CA
09 December 2017